Discovered In Retrospect

Sail A'non

Contents

ISBN: 0-9762941-7-6

Cover design and illustrations by Ömer Akın

Dedicated to

My Guardian Angels

Meral, Cem, Ayça and Mete Akın

My Father's Istanbul
June 10, 2012

Dear Dad,

When I was seven years old, you took me to Istanbul. In those days Istanbul cared; it made a difference how you conducted yourself. Lately, I've been reading your memoirs again and discovered that I learned most of what I know about this magnificent city from you. I am particularly taken by the section in which Uncle Hüseyin, the police captain, barred the door to your house with furniture and stood outside brandishing his captain's uniform and official issue revolver; in order to discourage vigilante hoards from searching the house for minorities. This is how he saved the lives of many Armenian and Greek families who lived on your street. Then, you too were seven.

So, during this trip, I decided to visit your old neighborhood even though these are very different times from those that you describe as: "it was a very difficult time for all, especially the minorities."

Your Son Ömer.

I arrived in Istanbul today. Tomorrow I need to take a bus to Ankara. After I checked into my hotel, I took the downtown shuttle. The road from the airport is different. Back in the day, it was a scarcely used four-lanner surrounded by ramshackle buildings, and empty lots. The traffic was slow, inundated with dilapidated trucks, and construction delays. Passengers who had the luxury of riding in a car were few and far between. The driver at the hotel remembers playing ball in the fields that have now gentrified into one of the most valued real estate property, on the globe.

The left side of the highway is lined with spanking new commercial and office structures interrupted only by well-manicured parks. On the right, the vista is deep into the Marmara Sea. It is peppered with merchant ships waiting to go through the Bosporus. Someone told me that the straights traffic exceeds 20,000 boats each year, and occasionally it takes months to gain passage. This has created a novel industry of small commercial boats providing all necessities of life, including women for the ex-patriot sailors sequestered on the big boats.

The guy sitting in front of me is conducting business from his laptop laid out on the seat beside him. He is a young, brash guy with manners that were undoubtedly honed in the service sector. His profile sports a hawkish nose and thick 5-oclock beard. He is carrying on with a heavy Eastern accent, bending someone's ear at the other end of his cell. He is oblivious to the disapproving glances of other passengers forced to move to the back of the bus on his account. After he is done, the absence of his high decibel volume leaves a palpable void in the air. As other, more distant cellphone conversations start to fill it; he remains oblivious to buildings falling off like playing cards on either side of the road. This seems like an auto-motor veil for his attention that is somewhere else, probably on matters of business.

Closer to the ancient city walls, the park near the shore is packed with people fishing and taking leisurely strolls. They are enjoying the mild-afternoon air by the sea and, despite the odds against them catching anything in the rushing waters of the Marmara, they are betting on earning their dinner from one of the rare freebies remaining for the inhabitants of this magnificent city.

The imposing walls and the gateway constructed with alternating layers of brick and stone defining our passage into the Old City look much too fresh at spots where they have been restored. After such a venerable territorial marker one would expect a dramatic change in the scenery; yet, it continues unabated. Overtime, current contrivances have overcome historic ones.

Soon we reach the Roman viaduct that now serves as the real gateway into the city. Here, the bus takes a left turn away from the shoreline and the scenery changes dramatically. Both sides of the road are lined with rows of 1950s style apartment buildings, stacked tightly against each other. They form long stretches, occasionally interrupted by a historic edifice, a piece of the city walls, or an institutional structure. The buildings are covered with a cacophony of signage announcing their commercial offerings: a porn store that is perfectly at home alongside banks, insurers, high school tutoring centers, tailors, and dentists. Rarely is there an indication that once these were all condominiums.

On the right, the mouth of the Golden Horn – an ancient riverbed which has become a waterway penetrating the bowels of the city – is flanked by ancient landmarks: the Covered Bazaar, Hagia Sophia, Blue Mosque, Topkapı Palace, Yeni Mosque, Süleymaniye, the Tünel (funicular) that connects

Beyoğlu to the Galata Bridge, and the Galata Tower. On the left, the Golden Horn snakes away, disappearing behind the hills across from the Pierre Loti Café and the former Ottoman tobacco factory constructed over the foundations of a Roman bath, which in turn was erected over ancient cistern walls. Unlike other world centers that appeal to the overhead flyby, Istanbul is a city of silhouettes. It is best apprehended on a boat or a bridge looking at one of its seven hills from a distance.

Now, we are on the Unkapanı Bridge. At the other embankment there are two derelict construction rigs towering over abandoned shipyards. The story goes that when the bridges were rebuilt, the planners did not take into account the height restrictions they imposed on boat traffic. This was years ago. Now the abandoned naval yards represent ugly tributes to boneheaded municipal officials and their benign indifference.

The shuttle climbs the Pera hillside towards Taksim, the city center. The snaking roadway moves us through a space sliced up by a myriad urban axes and accidents that are formed through the clash of building alignments and misalignments, gigantic billboards, vanishing streets, ghost imprints left behind by demolished buildings, and towering landmarks. This interesting confluence of visual impressions have been authored by a self-assured and enterprising mayor, who decided to cut through the spaghetti street pattern of ancient neighborhoods in order to create a six-lane roadway. Off of the bus I am like fish back in the sea. It has been years since the last time I was here and I observe everyone with a strange sense of longing.

A young woman as youthful and innocent looking as the girls I knew when I was going to college is scarfed and fitted out with a body length tunic, both symbols of the "Mild Islam" adjective attributed to Turkey by the West. As I drag my left leg with the help of my cane, a small man with cerebral palsy makes no attempt to meet my intentional glance. People carrying dark, stylish briefcases pass me by, engaged in business gobble-the-gook. Three business types, one woman and two men, all clad in sharp, black suits jaywalk but cabs do not honk their horns or move menacingly towards them like they used to do. Everyone acts with purpose and apparent indifference to their familiar environment. Children are notable only by their absence. They must be attending school where they, without a doubt, learn to be self-assured.

My boat ride is in the company of the same sort of people. Mostly young, some with scarves, and all with functioning cellphones. In Üsküdar, I first locate the bus stop in front of the mosque, which is the benchmark mentioned in your memoirs. I step precariously as I attempt to cross the street while paying much attention to the vehicles trying to meander between pedestrians and reciprocally too little to the uneven pavement in front of me. I badly twist my ankle that is still smarting from the Achilles tendon rupture it suffered last year. Even though this puts a damper on my already compromised stride, not to mention my spirits, from there on, it is easy to find the street on which your house once stood. The plan layout you drew in your book does not match anything I see on the street that bears the name in your sketch.

The old detached housing indicated has been replaced by 3-4 story attached, mixed-use buildings. A structure with wide frontage stands where your house would have been. Its first floor is a restaurant that is announced by a large billboard spanning the entire frontage. The name *Kanaat* (Contentment) seems to telegraph a serendipitous message urging me to embrace what I found rather than long for what I have yet to find.

It is a small, scarcely attended, mediocre eatery. I choose a table near a remote corner. As I am trying to pick the best of what's offered on the menu, two guys walk in: one, a macho brute with salt-and-pepper hair, a week old beard, and a full mustache. His shirt unbuttoned down to the waist reveals an excessively hairy chest. The other one is clean shaven, carrying a man-purse, and walking in the first one's arm. They sit at the table behind me. For no other reason than observing with clarity, I wonder if they are gay.

In Turkey, same sex companions walking arm in arm does not necessarily signal homosexuality. Also, carrying a man-purse is common. As I continue to eat, I try to avoid stereotypical conclusions that pop up spontaneously. This could be but a rare exhibition of out-of-the-closet behavior. After a while they leave with the guy in the other's arm complaining about how he is never allowed to pay. The macho guy reveals precious little about either sexuality or camaraderie. No one seems to take note of them, except me.

I trace my steps back to the boat dock, the funicular, Taksim Square, and the shuttle back to my hotel. Tomorrow, I'll be on my way to dull Ankara. I savor the moment by mentally revisiting the sights and sounds of the day. They are vaguely reminiscent of those I first experienced with you, as you must have when you first came to Istanbul as a refugee from Macedonia. In spite of the relentless "development" projects playing havoc with the delicate balance between what nature has provided in this enchanted land and what man has done to it, even the most intrusive and ugly structures erected in the past six decades fail to diminish the beauty of the Bosporus and Saray Burnu, its ancient peninsula.

"Gel buraya; gel bakim."

The adult companion of the shy kid, who must be about six or seven, leads him towards the captain-pilot of the intercity bus company. He has been beckoning the kid, who is wearing a cap with a "VIP" sign on it and showing signs of extreme shyness.

"Come here."

In order to engage him in friendly exchange, the captain-pilot picks the kid up and places him on his lap. "What's your name?"

"T..."

He pulls the kid's index finger out of his mouth. "What? My ears are not as good as they used to be. What?"

"What? Tolga?"

Kid's adult companion steps in to relieve the stress that seems to be building up. "I promised to get him some ice cream?"

The captain-pilot feeling a lack of closure insists on a conversation. "Who is this? Is this your grandpa?"

"Let me get him his ice cream."

As the rescued kid and his adult companion walk away, he speaks with apparent finality, "I'm his uncle."

There are forms of welcome intrusion in Turkey; and time and place when intrusion is unwelcome. I rarely see the latter, anymore. The kid, an unwilling participant in the exchange, who is about the same age as you must have been when you first set foot in Istanbul and I, decades later, at about the same age, nevertheless knew what we had to do even though it was not our decision.

Initially, the uncle was happy enough to indulge, but knew how to terminate it when the exchange became counterproductive.

Dear Dad,

I am on the bus now and am trying to concentrate on reading our favorite liberal daily. Its current editor who happens to be a parliamentary representative from the opposition party has been jailed for 1189 days with no relief in sight. He was placed under arrest for exercising his right to freedom of speech and to criticize the ruling party.

In the same issue, the paper reports that two university students have been sentenced to ten years in prison, for holding up a sign that said "give us free education." The paper argues that there is no reliable system of justice. Conflicts are acknowledged after the fact, when the act is deemed to be egregious by someone high-up.

The standard of care seems to be very different from the days when I was led all around town holding your hand. In this visit, I have neither seen any reminders of how a mere twenty year old police captain would put his life on the line for his neighbors, as did my Uncle Hüseyin, nor the youthful exuberance of an entire nation that once rose to combat injustice. People move with careless swagger bearing witness to selective insomnia of an honorable past and indifference towards a present full of promise.

Yet, it is a glorious day in Istanbul, with a deep blue sky peppered with a few white cotton balls. The air is comfortably warm cooled by an occasional breeze. This is what connects my senses with you across more than half-a-century.

Your Son Ömer.

I woke up with hopeful anticipation

December 2011

I woke up this morning with hopeful anticipation of what awaits: an agreeable breakfast, pleasant emails, a *New England Patriot*'s loss; or just a calamity-proof day would be just fine. I entered the family room where I had left my fleece jacket as well as my wife, son, and daughter, the night before. The jacket was hanging on the back of the rocking chair where I had put it. My wife, on the other hand is right behind me, rather than in her bed where I just left her.

It is 6AM. I looked at her standing, staring at me from the dark hallway behind me. When I made out her face through my smudged distance glasses I discovered a lovely smile. She does smile at me every morning, even before crows eat their droppings, but this is different. This is a broad happy smile with a gleam in the eye. "What? What's going on? Tell me!"

Lately, I have not had many pleasant surprises. One day in October I re-ruptured my Achilles tendon, just for walking to our dressing room, which was a repeat of the initial rupture I had in May, just for walking up some steps. Last year, almost to the day, December 22 to be exact, I was taken to the emergency room of the local hospital.

My older son constructed a Christmas tree for me from found objects in my hospital room. All of my maladies, of which I told you only half, came as surprises. I never expected my well trained, albeit slightly bruised Achilles tendon to rupture without provocation. I

17

never expected to have to stop at the stair-landing for several minutes, on account of a pulmonary embolism, as my son watched me breathe with a lot of difficulty. I never thought that my immune system, my bosom body, my ultimate defense, to attack me so viciously. Yes, I have been surprised a lot lately, but mostly unpleasantly.

I am hoping for something positive; her eyes tell me so, but her mouth is silent. Then with a roll of the eyes she points towards behind me and to the left. I turn around to "notice" after all of this, what would be obvious to anyone with some cognizance of their surroundings. It's the Christmas tree all decked out and sparkling with colorful lights. The note on the lampshade evidently addressed to me, says "you light up our lives."

Now this is a pleasant surprise! "We thought you might cry to see this," She says (I am crying just reading all of this, years later). "Not until I saw the note." I mutter. "I better go back to bed," she replies, still with a broad smile on her face. Even though it is two days after Christmas, this decked out tree is a reminder of all of my pleasant surprises.

My daughter and I share musings about literature, design, and life in general. She has turned into quite an elegant young lady with a head on her shoulders and a life partner of equal note. She lights up our lives every now and then, with a broad smile too. I wonder from where she got that smile and the gorgeous hair. She is one of my most pleasant surprises.

My younger son and I share a knack for research and writing. He turned out to be quite a scientist. He is there, unsolicited, to bring delectables prepared by his life partner Canan, or just to help with the daily chores. I have placed my personal healthcare on a day to day basis in his good hands. Despite his youthful stature as a doctor, that is one who can heal, he gives me sage advice. He is another of my most pleasant surprises.

My older son, the butterfly that hatched out of the cocoon when he was merely a teenager has taken the bull by the horns and pursued his dream to protect animals, to heal the earth. We shared the writing of a paper on creativity, illustrating of a book, and enjoying of Christmas trees when you least expect it. We even began to share some culinary moments together. He is yet another of my most pleasant surprises. As they say in the old country: "the horn exceeds the ear."

My greatest and longest lasting pleasure in life has been that young lady with the gleam in her eye, who is deservedly giving them a rest as I write these words. She has another long day ahead of her to clean, cook, carry, care, caress, and heal.

If there is a disappointment in all of this, it's yours truly, who sits around writing essays, causing trouble, and enjoying every surprise, pleasant or otherwise.

The Allegra Effect
June 30, 2009

"It's time for your sponge bath, darling!" The nurse yanked me out of my deep slumber. He has this annoying habit of pretending to be my sweetheart at the most inopportune moment. As I go in and out of consciousness, the Allegra Effect has been my best escape from life's malfeasance.

One of the first things anyone learns about commencements is that they are about beginnings and not endings. They mark the start of a new phase in the life of a graduate. What I found out during the last one I attended -- I must have attended dozens of them over as many years -- was that they are also about new beginnings for the parents. I am not speaking just about new horizons due to the ending of tuition payments, phoned-in mood swings, and career insecurities. I am talking about tangible personal growth through once-in-a-lifetime experiences.

I said: "Here, read this," as I reached over my wife's half of the table and handed the slightly crumpled envelope to my daughter sitting at the head of the table. She did not look puzzled as if she was expecting this. She started unsealing the envelope as my wife muttered.

"I thought we were going to write it together."

"I thought you told me to write it, owing to my talent with such things." I mumbled.

"But, I thought I would write something too." She raised her voice.

By now, my daughter the graduate, ignoring the tension in the air, had already focused her eyes on the small text I had printed minutes ago, on all the available blank space of the card, which simply had CON-GRADS embossed on its cover. Seeming overwhelmed with the length of my note, she said: "I will read this later."

"Read it now," I insisted.

After imperceptibly rolling her eyes, she decided to proceed.

I had just driven around Ann Arbor for over half-an-hour to simply find this lousy card. Trying to race in and out of the rain, I had spilled cold coffee all over my pants and shirtsleeves. I had sat at the local Subway sandwich shop, in an anonymous shopping mall, sipping Lemon Mist from a paper cup, just to be able to write these words of inspiration on her card. I was not about to be denied a witness to its reception.

"Read it aloud," my wife declared.

"Let her do it silently," I retorted.

She turned over the page. Her facial expression revealed none of the emotion I had poured into the card. I realized that all of the choice words I used sitting at the Subway booth, were platitudes and clichés. They seemed especially *out of place now, as we were staring at her at Sava. Just to compare the menus, not to mention my mood: Sava offered Omelette Mexicana for $12.95 while Subway, a Veggie Sub for $3.95. The Lemon Mist was already causing a minor havoc in my stomach and the omelet was yet to be ordered.*

"This note just got very; interesting." My daughter announced when she came to the part that pledged the much-anticipated $10,000 towards the purchase of her first car, which she pointed out to my son's girlfriend sitting beside her.

"Wow!" she said sounding sincere.

My son wanted to see it too, mostly out of self-interest. He is expecting to graduate in two weeks and to receive a similar gift. Finally, after a tense two days, doing all the things that families do at commencements, there was some contentment. But this too turned out to be a fleeting moment.

My daughter continued: "So is this what you have been doing for the past hour? What is this Subway anyhow? I didn't think Ann Arbor is big enough to have or need a Subway."

When I wrote those lines on the card, I had thought that it would serve as a bit of comic relief from the heavy pontifications I used in my essay. Obviously the literary license did not work. "I meant Subway, the sandwich shop."

"Oh, I see... You know dad? I have been worried-sick about you. Are you okay?"

"It's the Allegra he is taking," my wife interjected: "It made your brother tense, too."

Everyone at the table started chiming in with their two-cents-worth about the side effects of allergy and sleep medication they used at some point in time.

"Stop! I want to get off!" But I did not say it. Such emotions never help. You simply add more fuel to the flames of concern over your emotional instability.

"It is not Allegra," I said defensively, "I don't have any side effects from it. I have been taking it for a while. Come to think of it, it does give me cottonmouth in the mornings but that's all. You all know that your mom and I had an unusually quiet trip on the way up here and this is the side effect of that, and not some medication."

I knew my wife had been talking to the kids about my so-called unusual mood swings, so I felt obliged to explain. "In fact, she started it."

Everyone snickered. This is absolutely the worst way to explain away strange behavior. To compensate for the misstep, I elaborated. "She started the silent treatment and I am just sustaining it."

Words can never recreate our uneasy ride on the way up to Ann Arbor. They just make up new versions; versions that are never like the *original; versions that are new realities, or new originals that you have to interpret all over again. It is a never ending cycle, without beginning or end, just a relentless barrage of interpretations.*

"You mean you did not to talk to her for two days? Dad, I have never known you to. You know... You have had arguments before. Road rage is not unusual for you and mom. But you do not... I do not know you to let it interfere with things like your family's... with days like this... My graduation! I have not slept a wink last night, worried sick about you."

Since our family drives were always lively, it was particularly difficult for my kids to comprehend that we drove for 6 hours without a spoken word. Ordinarily we would have heated conversations; even sing songs.

The highlight of each voyage would be the 20-question game. Over the years each person had developed a 20-Question Game personality through their style of asking questions. Each of these corresponded to a character from antiquity. My daughter with skills of oratory is Cicero. My son, her twin, with his thoughtful and parsimonious queries has earned the nickname, Occam. My older son, the penetrating inquisitor, is Socrates. And my wife, waxing abstract about our interactions, would make an excellent Réne Descartes; yet I never had the motivation to tell them about these attributions. I can almost hear my wife objecting: "I think, therefore you aren't."

25

When did this turn out to be a dad's-having-a-nervous-breakdown thing? Is it just me acting strange? How about everyone else? Didn't anyone notice that my wife is not talking to me either? These thoughts did not occur to me until much later; so, I became defensive: "I sustained what she started; and it feels good."

Almost in an ironic move everyone became silent. My wife threw an oblique glance. My daughter was still puzzling over my uncharacteristically rebellious attitude. She is not accustomed to hear such statements from the man of family accord. I wonder what nickname I would earn in their estimation, perhaps Oedipus Rex, or worse.

She dug deeper: "If you felt good not talking, then why are you still acting weird; withdrawn into your shell, going off for hours with no explanation?"

"I am enjoying my newfound peace and quiet. I like it so much that I am trying to keep it up."

"Then why do you look so unhappy?"

"Well, I am upset too."

"I though you enjoyed the peace and quiet?"

"I do, but I am also upset."

"That doesn't make sense. Were you feeling happy or upset?"

"I am upset about making your mom upset; but I am happy that I found this zone of tranquility. When you do not talk you cannot argue. I have

been totally content for two days." I am definitely Oedipus Rex combatting my entire family clan.

So mom decided to set the record straight. "This is what happened; your dad was going on I-376, when I asked him to avoid the congestion and take I-579. He flipped out...... He ended up missing the exit..."

I have heard this before. "Okay, take this road; no, no, you should take the other one; wait! I just decided that you should take the original one; however, if what you say is correct, you must accept my original revision of course. Of course, of course..." I kept these thoughts also to myself.

"I just have had it. I do not want people interfering with my driving. I will not stand for it anymore." I said emphatically, "I have had it! I prefer to avoid all conversation just to avoid the interference."

My daughter was the first to articulate it correctly. "Are you saying that you have had an epiphany?"

"Yes, that's it: epiphany! That's what I had. Just keep quiet! Don't say a word. If you are going to argue, then it's better not to say anything."

I have a lot of explaining to do if I am going to dig myself out of this Allegra Effect thing. I can read in the faces of all around the table that this is the going conclusion. Who am I to disagree? I just feel a lot of empathy for people

who are falsely labeled "emotionally disturbed."
The more they protest, the more evidence they
provide that corroborates their alleged
condition.

My older son, Socrates, who is not with us at
the time, no doubt, will have a field day
dissecting this episode of our family
melodrama. I am not looking forward to
hearing his analysis.

I am not looking forward to the trip back home,
either. I have to choose between my newfound
freedom and the compulsory conformance to
expected family accord. So far, I am the culprit
for the headache and the Herpes attack that my
wife suffered on account of my passive-
aggressive conduct. The arguments have taken
their toll on her. Further, she is reeling from the
unpleasant prospect of being confined once
again into the tiny space of our sedan
accompanied by a silent partner, all the way
back home.

In a few weeks, my younger son Occam has to
look forward to several final exams and a gift of
the kind my daughter received. His girlfriend
has to go through the burden of driving him
back to Pittsburgh along with some of my
daughter's dorm-room furnishings.

My daughter, Cicero, is already looking forward
to enjoying graduate school, the $10,000
towards her new car, and an imminent trip to
the sunny South Florida beaches with her
boyfriend. I feel I have helped give her the gift

of knowledge, the freedom to explore new worlds, and the opportunity to own her car in which she can exercise her God-given right to drive the driver crazy.

"Take a turn right here! That is, unless you dare to disagree."

I opened my eyes and the nurse is looking at me with abject anticipation.

The Allegra Effect is fading away, but my mind is still preoccupied with ruminations of Socrates, Descartes, Occam, Cicero, and, yes, Oedipus. He has fetched two plastic tubs with warm water, couple of soap bottles, and a bundle of assorted towels to get to work on my crinkled and less than hygienic skin.

I smile at him with a blank stare.

Most Scary Halloween Costume
November 15, 2009

Traditional Halloween characters include the Devil, the Grim Reaper, ghosts, ghouls, demons, witches, goblins, vampires, werewolves, zombies, skeletons, black cats, spiders, bats, and crows. I decided to go as myself. Not that I'm cheap, trying to save a few bucks, or too lazy to think of an effective costume; I am convinced that the scariest one would be going as was myself.

I realized this when I was looking at the mirror, the eve of All Saints Day on November 1, 2009. I saw this average human specimen: balding at the top, with salt and pepper hair, puffy under the eyes, and a big belly; ghoulish, you might say in the dark of the night. What did a ghoul ever do to us that we would feel free to besmirch its good name by likening it to a human?

First of all, it is highly unlikely that you would ever meet one unless of course you have spent some time in the graveyards of Arabia. Check for yourself. Look it up in Wikipedia if you prefer. Here, I'll do it for you: "a ghoul is a mythological monster from ancient Arabian folklore that dwells in burial grounds and other uninhabited places." A ghoul is no more likely to hurt you than a Banshee, a Ch'iang Shih—a Chinese vampire – or Zeus, for that matter.

Ghouls abound in current Egypt. The graveyards in Cairo have been inundated by the homeless turning these serene and creepy environments into lively and functioning neighborhoods with running water and electricity. These poor souls are the creation of a far greater evil. Government policies that discriminate, economic systems that exploit the poor and police organizations that enforce capriciously are all created by people. And don't tell me these are well-meaning measures. They know exactly what is going on, and turn a blind eye to it in the interest of protecting their own stake in the status quo.

Cats, spiders, bats, and crows have done more good for the planet and other species than humans, with all their mighty tools, could ever dream of accomplishing before they cause their own extinction. Cats control the rodent population; spiders and bats control the insect population; and crows despite their human like ingenuity in using tools and displaying superior cognitive behavior, support nature's ecosystem as well as other animal species. New Caledonian Crows are the only known species other than chimpanzees, and of course humans, to make, select, and use tools to extract their food. Perhaps because of their ingenuity they have been demonized in more than one occasion, to wit, through their cousin the raven, by one of the great diviners of the human soul Edgar Allan Poe who says, in the last stanza of his eerie poem:

> *And the raven, never flitting, still is sitting, still is sitting*
> *On the pallid bust of Pallas just above my chamber door;*
> *And his eyes have all the seeming of a demon's that is dreaming,*
> *And the lamp-light o'er him streaming throws his shadow on the floor;*
> *And my soul from out that shadow that lies floating on the floor*
> *Shall be lifted – nevermore!*

This confirms my contention that the course of whatever evil we manage to attribute to other things, real or imagined, through our clever cognitive tricks, begins with human deeds. Is there any other species on the face of this small planet that plans, organizes, strategizes, builds tools for, and puts into action events that are intended to cause systematic extinction of its own kind, let alone other species, in the guise of spiritual, bodily, and communal satisfaction? The Barbarian Invasions, the Crusades, the 100-Year War, the 30-Year War, the Opium War, the Slave Trade, the First and Second World Wars, the attack on the World Trade Center, and the ongoing slaughtering of animals are but a few of our accomplishments.

Ghosts, ghouls, demons, witches, goblins, vampires, werewolves, and zombies in their singular efforts to scare and harm pale in comparison to any of these human achievements. Our efforts can only be compared to those of the Devil and the Grim Reaper, two characters that we invented in order to pass the buck. To add insult to injury, we undertake their missions effectively and then ruthlessly blame them; evil to the core.

I was still staring at the mirror, contemplating what to wear and how to bring out this particular human attribute. Should I place just enough *fond de ten* and eye shadow to subtly reveal the rot that is inside? Should I create a sinister smile with garish paint colors to blatantly conceal what is inside while revealing the manmade evil lurking outside? Or should I wear a mask that accentuates the true nature of humans?

This is when it occurred to me that I was perfect. I needed no accentuation, alteration, or re-framing to convey my intention. Humans have a long way to go to make amends to other humans, to other species, and to the planet. Until we do, it is best that we wear the naked truth on our outward appearance, without any aids or impediments.

Everyone thought that I was too lazy to think of and furnish myself with a costume, even though no one had the courage to say it. When I declared that I was perfectly scary as I was, it was met with consenting smiles, gestures, and cryptic utterances of approval.

Civility prevented contradictions from being offered.

The Talking Man
October 18, 2009

"Kick the habit and join the unhooked generation!" is one decade-old slogan that took a lot of concerted effort on the part of individuals, researchers, politicians, and health care officials to realize how trite a message it offers. But in the end, it helped wean most Americans from their smoke sucking habit beyond anyone's expectations. Today, the only way you can see smokers, as if they are members of an endangered species, is by going to a special viewing spot: the designated smoking area. Most buildings are smoke free. Even restaurants and bars are "clean" zones. Unless you smoke in your home, there are precious few options regular smokers to consume in comfort.

For a while, doorways and building entrances became outdoor smoking dens. These are the spaces easiest to reach outside of the official smoking areas. And smokers take an almost defiant pleasure to blow smoke, literally, in everyone's face as they enter and exit smoke-free buildings. Especially in inclement weather, smokers wrap themselves inside their trench-coats and clouds of smoke and try to stay warm for at least five minutes, even though it takes about seven at a leisurely pace, to absorb enough nicotine to last till the next break. Body heat plus the smoke condition microclimates in front of every entrance eave or porch. Non-smokers hurry through the plumes and huddling bodies so that they would not inhale more second-hand smoke than they have to.

The human figure with one hand stuck to the mouth has become a symbol of regression into habits that look and feel an awful lot like thumb-sucking. Surely there must be some Freudian explanation for this. In any event, this image of man, or woman, satisfying his, or her, most basic desires in broad daylight and under the guise of not-so-severe-an-addiction, has been a most convenient excuse for a most unacceptable behavior: sucking in public.

Rodin's "thinking man," on the other hand, has been the uplifting iconic image of humankind that befits our loftiest ambitions. In this case, the athletic male body made from bronze, resting his manly chin against his masculine fist propped up by his equally muscular arm gracefully resting on his knee, is engaged in deep though, presumably responding to his profound urge to think. He is satisfying his deep desire to figure things out, solve the never ending mysteries of human curiosity.

It has been a downer if not plain angst to have to think that, in the span of less than a century, we have descended from the pedestal of 'thinking" to covering under eaves. Yet, change is ever present. We have a new evolutionary phase emerging. Before, during, and after any event or assembly that requires an attendee's uninterrupted attention, people take breaks to talk. Now their hand is neither glued to their chin to think, nor their lips to smoke, it is glued to an ear to prop up a cellphone. We demonstrate an incredible desire to talk, to whomever we want, at whatever time or place, about anything at all, with no regard for whomever may be around us, anywhere, anytime, anyhow.

When did this desire exhibit itself in our past? Is it the neighborly chats around the fence gate, hanging around the neighborhood drugstore, or gathering around the cooler at work? No, this is a brand new addiction. We have very little interest in what is going on around us when we get that all important call from a co-worker, business deal, doctor's office, or someone in an emergency.

But wait, most cellphone calls are not these types of calls. We want to ask mom if this outfit I found at Macy's looks good on me. Quick, snap a picture, guess what, I can do it with the cellphone, which has now grown into a multifunctional device. I need to remember that ingredient in the recipe which I left on the kitchen table. I am too lazy to go upstairs to talk to you, oh I'll call you. And true story: I am too busy talking to you on the phone, so I cannot stop and chat with you even though I see you walking towards me. Since cellphones took over our lives, say about less than a few decade ago – incidentally, a little blimp in the evolutionary scale of humankind — our hands have been glued to our ears, our eyes to the cell-screen and our lips do not stop chirping.

You may wonder what happened to the emergency call which was the primary pretext for people to get these devices in the first place. We are still waiting for that technical glitch to be solved. It turns out that most 911 call stations are designed for landlines. As to the business call, it still survives among the plethora of unwanted commercial calls that each cellphone is inundated by and the increasing number of "National Do Not Call Registries" to which you must subscribe. But no sweat, just dial it on your cell.

It should be humbling to note that since Rodin made his thinking man in 1902, we have experienced two other principal states of evolution: the "sucking man" and the "talking man," both of which has brought out to daylight our innermost addictive tendencies revealed only through new technology: the modern cigarette and the cellphone. It is further sobering to note that the modern cigarette was made popular at the turn of the 20th century while the cellphone at the turn of the 21st. It took almost a century for cigarettes to be eliminated from our daily lives.

The safety of cellphones is a matter of debate these days. It may take a decade or two for the definitive findings to see the light of day since the phone industry would not relent until they develop the "safer" improved versions before conclusive findings would be available!

Two Tigers, One Rat, and a Strawberry Bush
October 10, 2009 *Inspired by an ancient Taoist story*

One fine morning, in order to revive my constitution and invigorate my mind, I decided to take a stroll in the woods. I am absorbed by my thoughts and the nature that engulfs me. However, soon I notice that I am being followed by a tiger. While the predator is at a safe distance, I am concerned that the coincidence in the direction of our movement might be more than just coincidence. Being the cautious man that I am, I hasten my pace. To my chagrin, so does the tiger. Little by little, my haste grows into panic and I find myself running as fast as I can, with the tiger in hot pursuit.

Suddenly, I come to a deep precipice with a valley below. Sensing that the eminent danger is becoming more acute by the second; I grab a nearby vine and start climbing down the side of the cliff. As I am feeling that my heroic exertion to save my life is about to pay off, as I descend the vine, I hear the now familiar panting of the tiger becoming louder not fainter. This makes me stop and look down. There is another tiger waiting for me at the valley below!

In spite of the fact that things are less than favorable, I think that I can wait out at least one of the tigers, if not both of them, only if I can conserve my energy and use the side of the cliff as a ledge upon which to settle some of my dead weight. This is when I notice that there is a new critter-sound in the air: the gnawing of a rat. My vine is being used as a filing instrument for the incisors of a rat that ruminates on the side of the cliff.

Could things get any worse?

43

At this moment of utter despair, I see a juicy ripe strawberry hanging off of a bush on the side of the cliff. It is within my reach. This is when all sense of danger and catastrophe leaves me. With a broad smile on my face, I pluck the strawberry and toss it in my mouth, savoring the sweet tart flavor and aroma of the fruit that has been prepared by nature for this singular opportunity, at this particular hour, on this particular fine day, for me to enjoy.

It is an abundant morning
October 14, 2009

My sneakers are cuddled by the cobblestones

They callused the hands of 200 year-old East-
Europeans

My fedora greets a dozen dormers that framed the
gazes of many sons and daughters of steel

I make my way to the lab,

hospital,

  studio,

    incubator,

      robot,

        bank.

I am challenged by the masses who built the

Second Industrial Revolution;

I am elevated by their presence.

There is an abundance of bridges,

blast furnaces,

  tanks,

    railroads,

      I-beams,

        cars,

          refrigerators.

(My spirit is lifted.)

I envision worlds that do not exist

gadgets that hear

    medicines that heal

        buildings that live

           energy that regenerates

I am one with the pioneers of steel and artifice

I have callused hands,

money,

    intelligence,

        the ingenuity of middle managers,

          I am East-European,

            I am Far-Eastern

It is an abundant morning in the 'Burgh

Death by Attrition
January 26, 2011

It is not the same as attrition by death. I think I read this somewhere deservedly obscure. All things start out by being alive, because they are formed by an unspoiled, pristine principle. Snow, for example, before people and cars muck it up, is alive. It covers everything based on the principle of gravitational attraction. Those surfaces that counter the direction of gravity are covered and the rest are not. Then little by little, motion, heat and chemicals transform it into a corpse. Tires smash it. Plows pile it. Sewer-line access covers melt circles in it. Salt particles pepper it with holes. Snow dies a thousand deaths before it vanishes and is reborn into another existence.

My friend the Oak Tree goes through the same process, only over a longer period of time, say a few centuries. Cardinals, roses, snails, ladybugs, and carnations all do the same thing within their own pace and pattern. Neither all animates are alive nor all inanimates dead.

Uranium 238 is not only alive but also fertile. Kim Jung Il, on the other hand, is as dead as a doorknob. For a long time, according to many indications, he ran North Korea – albeit with the help of Uranium 238 – which is a real feat for a cadaver. Even though with every passing quantum of time it tick-tocks closer and closer to its ultimate demise. The original constitution of 238 is intact and readily recognizable, even centuries later.

The sun is the most extraordinary of all living things. It lives a million lives and dies a million deaths every day. Every split second, it begins its cycle of birth on a new spot on our lonely planet, just as it concludes its cycle of death at a different spot far away. It is a metaphor for all living things that continuously light up and fadeout on the timeline of existence.

When I first began teaching at the Department of Architecture, I thought I belonged to a living thing. I perceived an order of knowledge acquisition and dissemination. The world was my repository from which I harvested. The students were my depository into which I deposited. Little by little I lost it all.

Kuhn convinced me that harvesting was a reenactment of an ancient Teutonic ritual. This is "embedded in our DNA and is a necessary part of a balanced life. Through ritual we are able to keep our Physical, Spiritual, and Mental aspects in dynamic balance." We go through predetermined motions of presumed discovery and end up with idea fragments, which are not alive, even for a second, and at best they are perfect candidates for a male-menopausal purge.

My protégé convinced me that he can imitate me and others, better than I could. He succeeded at success splendidly. He could think his way into deeper labyrinths of reasoning than anyone else. First he mastered depleting his constitution, and then he pulled the plug.

I wrote a poem for him.

As a reminder
I am writing a note to myself
He was soft spoken, confident, sensitive, passionate,
Cause he told me so

Like a quantum particle that oscillates now and then
He moved in and out
Little time for getting to know
Next time, I must remember that.

Little by little the constellation of lights that surrounded me got snuffed out by attrition. Each dying corpuscle of my being contributes in kind to this overall process until there is nothing left. This is the tirade I engage in every time I start lecturing during a new semester with a new bunch of students. Before I perish, I wait with bated breath to see if someone – anyone – will stand up and yell "bull shit."

Then it happened unexpectedly. They found my catatonic body in front of a whiteboard clutching a bloodied manuscript titled *"Death by Attrition, A brief Remembrance."*

The Coroner declared: "death by attrition, causing an offensively pungent decomposition throughout the environment." Since they could not identify the next of kin, they buried me in an unmarked grave close to the municipal dump. My casket was routed through Fairview Avenue for which I had written a poem in my days of biological vigor.

Eventually, my daughter Cicero inherited my bloodied manuscript that contains my poem. My wife Descartes is a clean freak. She would not be caught dead with notes of a bloodied sort. My sons, Socrates and Occam, have been too busy to be interested in trivia, while avoiding senseless carnage of man, beast, and all other creatures in between.

My mom, to whom I had dedicated my musings, could not be reached on account of her own demise, two decades ago, due to acute symptoms of the *Allegra Effect*.

The Oak Tree and the Flat Screen
November 21, 2010

Someone brought an oak tree into my sitting room,

Sporting massive branches and colorful foliage.

In a spiteful move, they placed her inside a measured frame, right above the flat screen TV.

The plane of the frame is turned a few degrees to the right to accentuate distinctions.

As if it is necessary.

The morning sun reflecting off of the glucose debris in each leaf lights up Christmas-like,

Festooned with so many tiny lanterns of maroon, gold and all that is in between.

Against the foliage, the bark on the branches glow in greens, yellows, and even blacks,

Like a sentry's gentle instrument, both protecting and nourishing the tree.

She's a sight to behold whether you are man or beast.

A designer, a carpenter, and a gardener have had a hand in the presence of our sitting-room guest.

No doubt the gardener wished to shade the sidewalk and the houses.

The designer positioned it just so, to suit the room's occupants and the façade to passersby.

The carpenter wanted a perfect frame and a well-crafted trim.

Humans are usually not this clever; unless their tacit instincts get the better of them.

As the morning colors assume an evening's solemn intensities.

As the fall composition becomes an *esquisse* of dancing limbs.

As wind songs make you aware of the gentle giant.

As the aroma of the blossoms, or the decaying leaves, fill the air,

The oak tells you a story of its making.

"How come you always stand there?" I need to learn more about this story.

"I just sway in the wind every now and again, which suits me just fine."

"How do you sustain yourself?"

"Humans work to earn their needful things; I scavenge. They store, prepare and consume food. They discard waste. So do I.

They do all of this by running thus a fro, hiding in rooms and houses, spilling refuse all over."

"I move as well, but very slowly: by twisting and turning, bending and swaying,

Extracting from the soil and giving more back to it,

Extracting from the air and giving more back to it,

Extracting from the sun and giving more back to it,

So as to preserve my good standing without disturbing more places than I need to."

"And you do all of this by just standing where you are? Holly molly!

Did you ever meet my son Socrates? You have the talk and he has the walk!

He is usually behind Starbucks where I once met Occam.

But I forget; you cannot go there, or anywhere.

Occam is all about 'doing the same with less;' the other day, a whippersnapper called him 'minimalist.'"

"Occam can never find anything in the garbage dumpster.

When he does, it is usually just a crumb.

The guy looks sickly like a razor, viewed along its edge.

I heard another whippersnapper call him 'anorexic.' I still have to look into this."

My tree friend is in quiet repose; Occam can learn a lesson or two from her.

Being the inquisitive guy that I am, I return to my inquiry.

"But don't you get bored? "

"I have the best view in the street; have you ever been up here with a thousand eyes?"

"Aren't you curious about other places, countries, planets?"

"I have travelled the world a few times over, and then some; the wind is my conduit."

"What about, reading books or walking dogs?"

She looked at me in painful contempt. Ouch! I can be thoughtless; I've been too close to humans.

"Doing experiments? Creating new things?"

"What do you think I do all day? Have you ever heard of chlorophyll?"

Doing all this without locomotion is quite a feat.

Our family room is endowed with a spectacle that is ever changing.

One that is deeply moving, broadly connected, and life regulating.

Always present without being indulgent.

Informative and interactive without monthly fees or annual contracts.

Not even a remote.

I look at the TV and ask what it has to say for itself.

It directs me to the remote, on which I have been chewing rather nervously for the last 30 minutes.

Most of the buttons are gnawed flush, all the way down to the surface of the instrument.

I have to use my nails to dig into them out.

Occam's Razor takes over; I decide to dose off into a dream about photosynthesis.

The Night Nurse
November 15, 2010

The nurse left the hospital at 5 AM.

He is wearing a hoodless, heavy parka, and black steel-toe shoes. All three are visibly worn out. With his crew cut, he resembles the naval types of the late forties. Given the proximity of the hospital to the marina docks almost makes him fit in. He takes a deep breath. The chilled, fresh sea air partially cleanses the taste of phenol inside his nose cavity. The hair in his nostrils seems to be hanging on to a few more molecules of the nasty stuff. He takes a deeper whiff. The rush of oxygen makes him dizzy. His right toe catches an errand paver and he stumbles on the sidewalk, keeping his balance with difficulty.

"Are you okay sir?"

"Yea, I'm fine." He says almost instinctively before turning around to see who it is.

She is one of the campus cops either beginning or ending her shift. Reluctant to engage her in a conversation of any length, at this time of night, he waves at her reassuringly and moves on. Owing largely to this brief exchange with the cop and the clumsy step that started his adrenalin rush all over again, he rides an efficacious gate all the way home to his condominium on Market Street.

By 5:25 AM he is already at the kitchen table, sipping his bedtime herbal-tea from his filter inlaid ceramic cup. This stuff has a calming effect on his constitution and helps him get more sleep in the waking hours of the morning. He is also nursing a sore left cheek bone with a pack of frozen peas he grabbed from the freezer. "Robin will not like this, I must remember to put it back before I go to bed," he thinks to himself.

It was about an hour and a half ago that Saeed attacked him with a plastic vase. Psychiatric wards do not have the glory depicted in the movies. Mental patients are not stenchless, noiseless, sensitive souls appearing as grainy images aimlessly pacing up and down in well-lit lounges. There are no heroes and villains; just hard work. And when things seem utterly normal, out of nowhere, you get wacked.

Ronnie is not going to like the bruise on Mac's face. There has been no time to treat it at the hospital. The altercation turned into a huge commotion. Saeed was wrestled by several attendants on the freshly waxed and slippery floor, with a thud that – now that he is reexamining the frantic events of the last few hours – undoubtedly came from his forehead hitting the floor. Blood was everywhere. They sedated the poor bastard and strapped him down in the OR for the surgeon on call to stitch him.

When he left, Saeed was still in the OR. He is a casualty of the Iraq War. Conflicted about his nationality and ethnic origin and severely injured by shrapnel he received in the skull nearly three years ago. Initially shuffled from one VA hospital to the next, he finally ended up at the Old Dominion University Hospital in Norfolk. He has not able to reach a stable mental condition. His father, a refugee from Lebanon in the 60's, lived nearby Sugar Land, TX, which made his move to Galveston sensible.

Saeed's father is a short, bearded, bald, and fat man. He is dedicated to his son, as there neither appear to be a mother, who is alive or available, nor siblings who visit. His father, however, comes to visit three times a week. Each time he brings an audio tape of a literary work narrated by a well-known American or British actor and an old fashioned portable tape player, all tucked away in his vinyl shoulder bag of 60's vintage. They sit in Saeed's room and listened to the tape for about 45 minutes or so, before he leaves. This week's docu-novel is Isaac's Storm, the great Galveston flood, at the turn of the century. Since bedroom doors have to remain ajar when there are visitors, all passersby can hear the narrative broadcasting from Saeed's room and some pause to follow parts of it: "*The system, he told Congress, helped explain why Weather Bureau employees had to be committed to insane asylums more often than employees of any other federal agency. He said this with pride.*"

After all these many years in the US, Saeed's father, proprietor of a Middle Eastern grocery store in Sugar Land speaks only basic English. On the other hand, having been born in the US and acclimated to the culture around him at a very early age, Saeed spoke perfect English but broken Arabic. After all with the frequency of the visits there was very little new stuff to talk about; and narrated novels turned out to be a suitable pastime for both father and son.

Each time, their farewells were almost the same. "You look good today. Keep up the good work. I'm proud of you. Bye."

Saeed seems oblivious to the loaded emotional content of these simple exchanges. Owing mostly to their repetitious, cliché content the words delivered with passion by the father are either lost in the corners of Saeed's disheveled mind or deliberately tuned off.

"Okay baba!"

"See you later, son"

The final goodbye exchange usually enacted near the reception desk of the ward on the third floor elicits, at best, an affirmative mumble from Saeed.

Talk about a relationship full of holes and a poor, old man constantly trying to fill them up with the force of sheer emotion. No doubt that the bonds between these two broken men once ran deep and were fortified with wholesome familial ties. Now it seems to lay in ruins, ill-nourished in a landscape of dubious heritage. It all seems like a scenario played out by authentic and desperate Hemingway characters embattling their tragic destiny.

This morning, still smarting from his painful shiner, Mac has little to no sympathy for Saeed, whether a Hemingway character or not. It is 6:05AM. Ronnie's alarm will go off in 25 minutes. All of a sudden Mac feels the full weight of the expiring night's toil and trauma. He still has to put away the tea cup, the soggy bag of peas and climb into bed.

He goes into the bedroom; brushes his teeth. His facial bruise does not look too good. He is glad Ronnie will not notice it in the dark of the early fall morning. He changes into his pajamas efficiently and crawls into bed with him.

A few minutes of quality time in the morning is what he needs to calm his nerves. Ronnie is still asleep. Mac snuggles from behind and caresses his chest moving rhythmically under the respiratory pace of REM sleep. Ronnie turns around and hugs him affectionately.

"Hello Doc," he whispers under his breath.

"Bye, professor," he retorts.

As their state of consciousness swaps over during the next twenty minutes, Mac will remain peaceful and alone in bed for the next six hours.

By the time Mac has to return to the hospital for his new shift, it is 7PM. He is in a good mood. Around an hour ago, during their quick bite for supper, Ronnie was more than sweet about his swollen left cheek bone and eye. Mac is well rested from a good night's sleep and expects a quieter time at the hospital. Often, the tension in the psych ward will build up like in a pressure cooker until it is released with a blowout of some sort. Then things are fine for a while. Yesterday's commotion will most certainly have a calming effect on things today.

Indeed the lobby of the hospital seems unusually quiet especially for a Monday morning. Mac decides to walk up to the ward. Once he is on the third floor lobby, the first thing he wants to do is to check-in on Saeed. But he finds his room to be vacant. He decides to walk over to the reception area, which, curiously, he finds to be full of people. Nurses, administrators, and strangers assembled in clusters are conversing quietly. As eerie as it seems, this explains the relative calm and quiet elsewhere in the hospital.

As Mac approaches the reception desk he recognizes the officer from the night before, standing at the opposite end of the lobby area. He begins to walk towards her when he notices Saeed's father out of the corner of his swollen eye. He looks almost formal, wearing a tweed jacket, a white shirt, and a clumsily tied brown tie. He has shiny black Oxford shoes with grey socks and dark grey trousers hanging too high over his shoes. He is surrounded by a group of foreign looking young men all of whom have their gaze fixed on Mac.

"Are you Mac?" Saeed's Father asks.

"Yes," Mac replies instinctively.

"I came to take my son."

These words rolling out of his mouth, at first, with uncharacteristic speed, get stuck somewhere between his throat and his heart, which is where he places his fist with implied force.

"Are you Mac Golding?" The officer whom Mac was trying to reach must have overheard the conversation, and was now standing near him.

"Yes, I am."

"I need to ask you a few questions," pointing the way to one of the vacant patient rooms.

The patients must have been moved to a space away from the residential block, which is the standard practice at times of high distress. As they walk past Saeed's father and his young companions Mac notices that everyone is staring at him.

He stops, turns around, and, almost defiantly, engages the laser sharp stare of this small old man with whom he had never exchanged even a single word all these years, let alone make eye contact. At this moment, he looks smaller, older, and utterly evincible. His bloodshot eyes are full of an unmistakable look of desperation and puzzlement often present in his son. The only difference is that they have turned into two dark and bottomless wells of grief.

Suddenly, Mac becomes aware of poor Saeed's demise. Overwhelmed by a reciprocal and unavoidable feeling of sorrow, he finds no words to speak. He turns away from the old man and follows the officer into the empty patient room for his debriefing about last night's events.

Is it Real or A Reel?
January 26, 2011

"You are so cheesy. Where did you come up with that lame line? I bet you heard it in a Spaghetti Western."

Chucky objected: "No it was not a Spaghetti Western. It was in some lame Turkish movie script I came across on the web."

"Aha, so you admit it is lame."

"No I don't admit to no such thing. Some of the lamest scripts have the best lines." Chucky transitioned into one of his forgettable imitations of Clint; "C'mon make my day!"

"C'mon snap out of it Chucky. I tell you that my D'Artagnan died and you give me cheesy Clint imitations."

"Wait a minute. Clint isn't cheesy."

"I know he isn't; it's you who makes it cheesy."

"Sorry, Cappuccino I can be insensitive sometimes…. especially when I am so full of cinema… How did your dog die?"

"I don't know. I did not see him. I was told that the Coroner declared it '*death by attrition resulting in offensive decomposition of the body.*' They buried him in a tiny grave at the municipal dump. I have only one memento left from him; this tattered manuscript: *Death by Attrition, A brief Remembrance by Espresso,*" into which he has been chewing compulsively.

"Hold it; hold it; wait one frocking Romero minute! Who are we talking about here? They don't burry people, not even mares, at the municipal dump; even if they are zombies."

"Zombies are real people who happen to be dead. They rise from proper graves, you know... Not from garbage dumps."

"Here you go again talking movie crap. I'm talking about my dog, you idiot. Dead; butchered by villainous treachery, I'm sure. There are splatters of blood on the manuscript."

"He must have been attacked viciously by an evil swashbuckler." Chucky snapped out of his zillionth moment of embarrassment and slid right into a Scaramouche imitation.

"You may turn your back on Scaramouche, my lord, but surely you will not run away from Andre Moreau!"

Then he snapped back to reality just as seamlessly. "He was a four legged, wet tongue. He was not your relative."

"He was too."

"No he was not."

"Yes he was. I adopted him."

Chucky looked at me with that familiar gleam in his eye. This was the telltale sign that he was going to come up with a movie script line that would fit the moment. So I cut him off.

"D'artagnan and I became very close after my mom and I were confronted by zombies, many moons ago."

"You know canine are very sensitive to the full moon, so D'artagnan and I, to listen to the lamentations of lonely canine, always went by the lunar calendar."

Before Chuckie could even get a gleam in his eye, I continued.

"One fateful day, I was wearing my neatest outfit and brand new leather sandals. I can still remember the chickadee-clacks of my heels, my rosy cheeks and my taffeta skirt. Then out of nowhere appeared D'artagnan."

"I said to my mom 'Mommy what's wrong with this dog? He has crappy hair.' My mom said 'That is not hair dear, and she is not crappy.' Then one thing led to another and D'artagnan growled at my mom ... come to think of it was more like a slurp. Then my mom took out her cell and D'artagnan high tailed it from there before she could call 911. This is how we made his acquaintance."

Chucky sounded puzzled. "That does not sound like an auspicious encounter. How come you adopted him?"

"I don't know, why and how but the next time I saw him I was being harassed by Expres-son."

"You mean Lardass Express."

"Yes, that's him. He added a "–son" after his surname to make it sound chic."

"Despite his pretentions, he was nothing but an obnoxious Lardass. He kept bothering me every time I had to walk to the bus stop alone.

That is until that day when D'artagnan showed up. He put his right paw on Expres-son's right shoulder and with the left paw gave him a quick punch in the jaw. You can never imagine the trepidation this caused Lardass. First, he had no idea what had happened. Then, he turned around only to see this mangy creature staring him down with two paws on his waist; his shoulders pushed way down and his wet tongue sensing the fear emanating from Lardass. That was the last time Express-son bothered me but not the first time D'artagnan rescued me from threats."

"He was always there like, like Steward Granger or Errol Flynn …" Chucky continued "Tyrone Power, Burt Lancaster, Basil Rathbone, Douglas Fairbanks, Sr. and Jr.,.. "

I had to stop him before he relapsed into his usual Cinema-litis ailment: "yes, yes we get it. So that's how I adopted him, without signing papers and such."

I looked at him with marginally feigned incredulity. You see, Chucky is a cinema buff; he can be dense when he is in a trans; but usually he is pretty smart. He wants to be a film critic someday. In order to advance his career opportunities he is even willing to call himself a "movie" critic before he gets the job.

Since 4th grade, at times when he should be at school, he has been spotted coming out of movie theatres and alone! Some thought he was a perv. The reality is that he is a cinema-perv. Once he convinced his mom that school was open on President's Day so he could attend the premiere of "President's Day."

Chucky asked me if he could look at the chewed up manuscript I inherited from D'artagnan. He told me that I should try to turn some of these chronicles into movie scripts. Coming from him, even though he is not a film critic yet, it felt good.

Having found several meters of discarded cellulose acetate among coke cups and popcorn boxes, we called it a day, and quietly left the dumpster area behind the theatre.

Reading to Art
March 25, 2012

"She closed the book, placed it on the table, and finally, decided to walk out the door for the last time." She was sure that she had read this quote somewhere. It was either in *Alice* or *Knights of the Round Table*. With all of the reading she had done recently, she could not be sure.

For the last several months, reading had become second nature to her. Ever since Art passed away, and even before then, she has been reading aloud, first to him and then to herself. When she read to him, she presumed that Art enjoyed listening to the tone and the special cadence she developed in her voice. She believed that it calmed him down; reduced the involuntary thrashing of his limbs; and even lulled him to sleep. After he was gone, she was no longer sure if it was not all in her head. Doctors had assured her repeatedly that his motions were involuntary and he was unable to hear or understand what was going on around him.

In spite of this, she continued to read to him selections from his library of fiction. She created a special set of novels that she carefully chose from the ones that he liked, the ones that they read to each other before his accident. She selected ones that had a significant character named Arthur. She even converted some names to "Arthur" by going through and writing on the pages of the text; for fear that she may slip and say Ishmael, Heathcliff, or Mulligan. She believed that hearing his name persistently and compassionately, Art would reciprocate reflexively, if not consciously.

Even after the removal of the medical equipment and the abatement of the smell of terminal illness from the room – which she had come to accept, even look forward to, in her desperate mission to be one again with Art – she kept on reading without missing a beat. The sessions without him, assumed a life of their own creating a sense of serenity and solace for her. This is how her healing began.

These solitary sessions were a mere continuation of a habitual act. First, she sat in her rocking chair near where the hospital bed used to be and cried until she was drained of emotion. The stillness of the room evoked a kind of incompleteness. Then she read slowly and deliberately. As the minutes turned into hours she often found herself orating in the hallowed ground of the library like Cicero fighting for his life. Then, her voice would become solemn as if it was the conscience of thousands of book spines surrounding her in astounding stillness. And even though she would have no idea what she was fighting for, she would fear that breaking the chain of these reading sessions would signal something calamitous. So she kept on reading, as if he were still in the room, consuming, devouring the remaining volumes of the collection that was originally created for Art.

Recently, these events became an emotional life-vest for her, easing the pain of her loss by revisiting memories and forming new ones. She became resilient, even content, feeling that as she neared the completion of these readings a momentous closure for her would be at hand.

As if it was the fulfillment of this prophecy, one day, Art's library, quite spontaneously, transformed itself into a shrine for all of the expired souls in the volumes it contained. She felt self-assured that the next time she walked out of its door; she would not have to come back once again.

Bowling with Sunflowers
June 30, 2009

Caught up in the excitement of my clandestine mission, I parked my bike a short distance away and entered the sliver of space between the two adjacent lots. Filled with haste and trepidation, I made my way on all fours, between the autumn-dew covered sandstone wall of the police station and the all-purpose bushes separating the two properties. My hands were catching candy wrappers, champagne corks, and plastic toy-parts. I was glad I still had my biking gloves on.

As I made my way closer to the tall, gently-inclined sunflowers, two shadows emerged from the police station. A jolt of cold shiver ran down my spine when they stopped only a few yards from where I was. I froze like a cat considering risky options; my right hand hanging by marionette strings belonging to the dense, dark, geriatric night-air; my left palm buried into something mushy. A sense of panic followed my shivers. I was precariously close to hyperventilation. A loud guttural sound would be the last straw to upset the delicate balance between the predawn hush and my overworked nerves.

Once my reason returned from its paranoiac vacation, I began to consider. The house to my left is on my morning walk to school. For the past two months, five days a week, I have been noticing the tall, lanky, gorgeous-looking sunflowers, in its front yard. Each morning, I also notice a woman and three children of consecutive years of age, leaving the house-with-sunflowers.

81

She looks like a bowling-ball with sticks as limbs and a tiny golf-ball for her head. The kids are similarly proportioned, loud, and hyperactive. Every morning they lumber erratically towards the bus stop.

I hate fat, short, stubby, loud, hyperactive kids just as much as I love sunflowers. Soon after, I began to see nightmares of chubby little hands bowling delicate, fresh sunflowers, into gigantic saliva-filled apertures. From there, it was only a small step to deciding to rescue the defenseless, innocent delectables -- even if it meant stealing them in the dark of night.

This is how I got into this pickle.

It had gotten light enough for me to clearly see the features of the two cops who were still exchanging notes about their morning shift. It was only a matter of time before they would be able to see me, as well; and in my compromised position. As I fathomed this exceedingly inconvenient possibility, one of them kneeled down to unleash her canine companion. At that moment, I found myself exactly at eyelevel with her and closed my eyes, not daring to stare for fear that she may sense my gaze. Then, instinctively, I leaped up, turned around, and started running towards my bike. In a flash, my brain had calculated that the risk of my mission was too great for the prize I was seeking; while at the same time it had miscalculated the superior sense and speed of my pursuer. Seconds later, I was wrestled to the ground with two powerful paws pressing me down and stinging canine teeth embedded in my buttock.

The police postponed my debriefing until after I was joined by my dad, at the local clinic, where I was being treated. It was not easy to convince anyone, let alone my dad, of the truth of my innocent motive, especially while lying on my belly revealing a bandaged buttock.

"You mean to tell me, you were just stealing sunflowers."

"Why didn't you just buy some?"

"Do you realize that this is wrong?"

 "You look like a smart kid, " and so it went.

All considered, I believe, I got off easy: 30-days of community service under my parents' supervision. I did my service by collecting signatures for a permit parking petition for our street. The house with the sunflowers was on my signature route. One afternoon, I approached it, not knowing if the owner knew of my misdeed. The bowling-ball lady opened the door.

"I am collecting signatures…"

"I'm sorry, the owner is not here. Can you come back later?"

Months later, on Halloween, I met the owner of the house. He was handing out Banana Sunflower Seed Cookies which everyone believes he bakes himself. Apparently, he is a chef at a gourmet restaurant in town. Mercifully, soon after, my nightmares with obnoxious kids mangling fresh sunflowers with their dirty, stubby fingers came to an end.

84

He Looked Old
Summer of 1986

His balding head and wrinkled face attested the passing of too many emotions in less than commensurate number of years. He pushed on, almost oblivious to the burden of the companion on his back, and limping around boulders and smaller rocks littering the river bed. Further up the slope, he adjusted his load consisting of a set of amorphous bundles attached to his body through miscellaneous wires, tubes, and ropes, with a jerking motion. This seemed to both lighten the familiar weight tugging at his shoulders and appease the bundle on his back.

The mountain in the distance looked formidable. He was not sure if he would make it all the way to the top but he pushed on all the same. While his motions were self-assured, his face revealed a sense of insecurity. With the familiarity of a tight rope walker, his feet found smooth stable surfaces, avoiding crevices between sharp rock clusters. With every step he shifted his load from one side to the other he exhibited the assurance of an elephantine lumber with the elegance of a gazelle's tip-toe. He was making slow but steady progress.

Far ahead, the river bed disappeared into dense vegetation before emerging beyond a grove of trees as a shimmering reflection. The white caps of the mountains feeding the river with fresh melted water were visible beyond the greenery. It was early June and the snow cover still remained just below the rocky protrusions of the mountain top and further below.

When he started climbing several weeks ago at the foothills surrounding Lake *Erhai*, he did not anticipate that he would be this far along his path, so quickly. He could have done even better if he were alone. He jerked his load up with familiar, almost instinctive motions, realizing that he had not been alone for as long as he could remember.

As he moved on, the riverbed got narrower and deeper leaving only a skinny path of dry rocks on either side. With water splashing with the force of the river's flow, the dry moss on the rocks had become wet in places and made for a precarious progression for his normally secure foothold. He decided to move away from the river bank but not before he would refresh his hot and sweaty body with the cool crisp water running right beside him.

He carefully stepped onto two rocks projecting out of the river surface just at the right distance from the edge of the water. By gradually bending his knees and leaning forward he brought his body closer to the water surface, carefully balancing the grotesque shape he and his companion constituted, on the two rocks upon which he was standing. The traction under his feet was good enough.

He leaned over and cupped some water from the river with one hand and brought it into his mouth. The water he splashed into his mouth was slightly salty owing to the sweat that had accumulated in his palms, reminiscent of previous times when he was in similar situations. He decided to go down on his hands and knees and try to gulp down as much water as he could without having to splash it all over his face.

He hated the drips of water hanging on to his moustache since this required him to use one arm to manage the entire load on his back, while wiping down his face with the other hand. Almost out of necessity he began to enjoy the cool water droplets running down his long moustache onto his chest. He was content.

As he raised his body and his load above the surface of the water rushing around the two rock embankments, he cut a strange and graceful figure like Nijinsky dancing the "Right of Spring." Looking ahead he raised his eyes towards the rock immersed in the river just in front, with a sheet of water gliding over it. For a moment he stared at the dark reflections on it with eddies circling around it. They were expressionless at first; then, for a few seconds, a glimmer of sarcasm flashed over them before it disappeared altogether, overtaken by the hopelessness that preceded it.

He carefully got up and moved away from the riverbed onto dry land with mounds of rounded rocks. Once again, he tried to adjust his load as he progressed on the uneven surface. Each time he tried to shift his load from one side to the other, his energy depleted by his arduous climb, he looked less graceful and more like a Sumo Wrestler in a defensive stance.

Once he reached the end of the rocky embankment he found himself at a grassy bank abutting brush-land at the edge of a forest. When he reached the forest, the trees parted and engulfed his hot skin with it's cool and breezy shade. As he disappeared into the shade of the trees, the radiant heat surrounding his body began to blend with the fresh, forest air.

He came to a patch of the forest marked by three trees: a pine and two sycamores. He chose one of the sycamores which had a fallen tree trunk right beside. He approached it and turned his back towards the tree trunk resting on the grassy ground. He started to kneel down just, as he did at the river bed a short while ago, but this time shifting his center of gravity backward towards the log. With a gentle release he landed the bottom of his load on the log and his own bottom on the grassy ground near it.

He looked relieved. He started working on the buckles, wires, tubes and ropes connecting the suit covering his body to the body of his load. With a few familiar twists and turns he freed himself from his suit and faced his load, now listlessly seated on the log. It looked like a humanoid: a dwarf or an amputee bundled in a sac devoid of expression.

He needed to ask, "How are you feeling?"

The retort was curt, "Why didn't you let **me** drink?"

"Because it may harm you in ways we do not yet understand."

"Then why did **you** drink?"

It was almost as if a mechanical diaphragm had opened and closed revealing an abacus-click, concluding a preprogrammed response. Nothing more was said. There was a quick flash of anger on his wrinkled face that was quickly overcome by an expression of calm. He tried to encourage his companion, as in so many other times, to be open and trusting. But his words were always ineffective. So he said "as you wish."

Their eyes met in tacit disagreement. The old man was seeking acceptance of his age and experience. He wished to be taken at his word. He wished to pass on something of value to his companion. He had come to appreciate tradition, which came to him in the expected way, through experience. He wished to communicate this but they were at an impasse. As if in a Bridge game, each one was trying to outbid the other getting dangerously close to a point of no return.

He did not even want to contemplate the end game. There was no option but to push on. He crawled back into his contraption twisting and turning to balance the load onto his back. He started to attach the buckles, wires, cables, tubes and chords carefully. There was a sense of unease in his posture but his moves were as calibrated and sure as that of a skilled surgeon. When all was reattached and his load was firmly positioned he began to lean forward. A feeling of warmth began to overtake his neck and his shoulders.

He knew he was a prey once again.

Owning the Street
July 15, 1992

I first noticed it one early morning while I was waiting for the bus. I had plenty of time since apparently on Sundays the "early" bus did not run and the next bus was at 8AM. I had nearly two hours to kill and there was precious little going on in the suburbs of *Thessaloniki,* at 6 AM on a Sunday.

Mercifully someone showed up at the other end of the street walking towards me. She was dressed all in black including black stockings and a black babushka over her head. Her black shoes seemed like a new-fangled version of comfortable peasant clogs, likely cast from a composite of fabric and polymers.

Her steps were measured and brisk. She must be in her late fifties. Her wrinkled face and the gray hair that framed her face from under her babushka contradicted her energetic and youthful stride. All of her garments fit her perfectly but with some accommodation for the moving parts. Her one piece dress was tied at the waist with a black, fabric belt.

I was reminded of women that I saw in Italian movies of 50s and 60s. It occurred to me that she must be going to church I had noticed the day before that is located in the direction she is heading. My suspicion was confirmed a little later when first an old man and then another woman started heading in the same direction. Dressed in his best Sunday clothes he was making slow progress with the aid of a cane.

The other woman was younger and dressed in identical clothing as the first woman. She was overtaking the older gentleman.

As she passed by him, they exchanged words in Greek. She seemed to be greeting him and inquiring about his state of wellness. When he replied, she stopped as briskly as she had been moving. Her fists were placed on both hips and she appeared to be addressing him sternly. Yet, there was no particular anxiety involved rather it was either part of her abrupt personality or her Sunday frame of mind. In fact one could easily see this as a frank and friendly exchange.

This is when I noticed that she had planted her feet plumb in the center of the street as if she owned it. This seemed contrary to modern vehicular traffic protocol. What if a car showed up, perhaps someone else going to church? Would there be enough time for her or the old man to move aside? The car would have to go around them, making for a very strange traffic circumstance. Until today, I had not thought of our relationship to traffic in these terms.

This morning I woke up in *Ürgüp it was* much too early. The adrenalin accumulation in my body from the activities of the previous days of travel and the fact that I went to bed too early the night before made me rise early. I decided to leave my wife and the kids in bed, at the motel, and take a quick stroll through town. I walked out of the front door of the motel complex and started upslope on the street that snaked between buildings the left. The street was surfaced with cobble stones and lined with traditional Anatolian houses with courtyards, garden walls, and their main axis aligned in the North-South orientation.

The houses in the entire town were constructed with soft volcanic stones quarried in this area for centuries. Hence, at first glance, it was difficult to distinguish the new from the old. By some accounts, this area has been inhabited continuously for more than 4,000 years. The volcanic ash covering the whole region has provided a flexible palette for construction, both with houses built from quarried tuff as well as cave dwellings carved right into mounds of tuff.

Inhabitants of the area continue to build using similar methods, adding new house design versions to the existing repertoire of diverse urban forms. The entire composition is flexible enough to accept new house types without sacrificing from the integrity of the entire environment and sufficiently restrictive, due to the limitations of constructing with tuff, to maintain a consistent language of building.

As I was absorbed in these thoughts, I came to a fork on the road marked by a fountain carved right into a wall of tuff. I continued on one of the streets moving away from the fountain. It was flanked on either side by older structures evidenced by the presence of debris, neglect, stillness, and the mannerism of their inhabitants. I wasn't sure how old I could go back in history without thinking about the early Christians who took refuge here hiding from the Roman soldiers, which, by the way, accounts for the catacombs carved into the ground, at places, six tiers deep.

While returning to the motel, I noticed I was walking on right side of the street. It was early enough in the morning to not worry about risk of running into vehicular traffic, yet, by force of habit, I seemed to be sticking to the sidewalk zone.

This is when it dawned on me that instinctively I did not behave as if "I owned the street." There and then I decided to walk in the middle of the street, swinging my arms, looking at the buildings to my right and left and not having a care about traffic. I proceeded with a sense of, at once, owning the road and belonging to it.

This is the way it must have been many years ago when motor vehicles were introduced to the urban street that used to be *owned* by carts, carriages, horses and pedestrians. Before that period of transition, the street did belong to the pedestrian, like the emperor in the Forbidden City owning the central path connecting all of the significant edifices.

There was accommodation for all to own a piece of the street *commons*. Amicable acceptance of mutual ownership gave form to equitable, timeshared or even hierarchy-ordered ownership of the street. It made for a civilized sharing of the commons.

With the introduction of the motor-vehicle into the mix, and the invention of the sidewalk, the road no longer belonged just to the pedestrian. Today it mostly belongs to the motor-vehicle. With the assistance of traffic engineers we timeshare the patch of pavement called the pedestrian walkway, regulated by green yellow and red lights.

Unless one dares to chat with one's neighbor, in the middle of the road, on the way to church, and with both fists resting on the hips; woe to the driver who dares to run you over. Red light or not, the pedestrian willing to take a risk with their life or limb can still own the road.

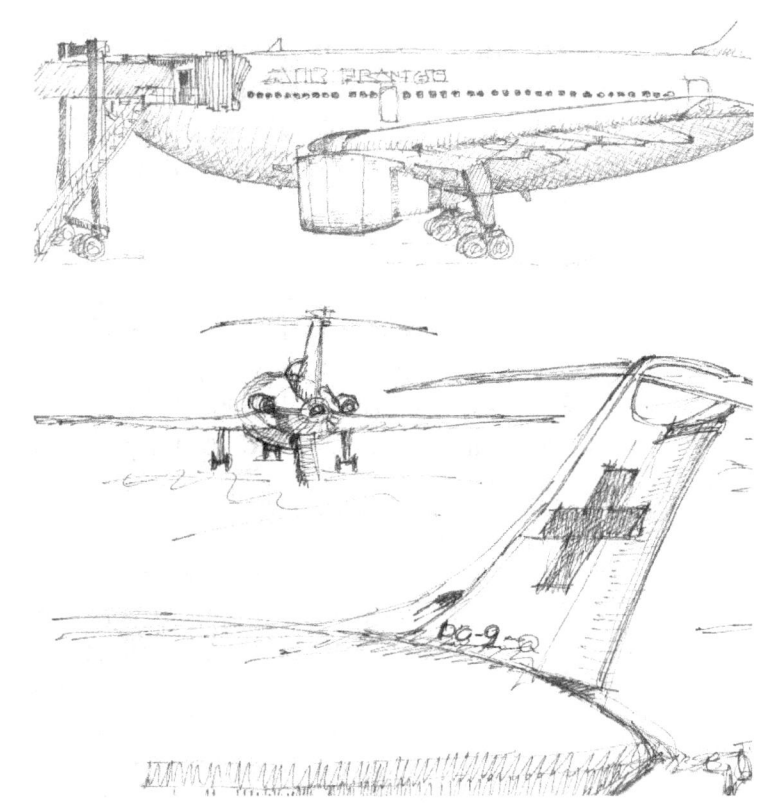

It's a Wondrous Sight
March 23, 1985

As I peer through the porthole, the lower portion of my visual field is almost entirely taken up by the top face of the wing. Its forward edge is a sweeping line extending all the way from the lower left corner of my visual field to the upper right. The engine hanging below the wing is almost perfectly horizontal. While force of its thrust evokes ideas of masculinity its curvilinear shape embodies an aero-sensuous notion of fetish. Perhaps, having spent three intense days in Saudi Arabia, my poor brain is no longer capable of apprehending notions without referencing gender specific adjectives.

Beyond the wing I see distant clouds. In front of the nose of the jet there are particles of white cotton balls and a horizontal streak of white stuff. All of this is set against a deep hazy blue sky that gradually turns into clear blue through the modulation of thousands of subtle hue variations, as if choreographed by a magician's hand.

The wing of the plane now occupying a vast portion of my visual field is made up of dull grey aluminum-alloy sheets riveted securely to its structural frame. The rivets are lined up methodically into rows parallel to its visible edge. This pattern is interrupted by round or rectangular patches of aluminum that must serve as access points into the wing cavity. Now the chaotic layout of patches and different hues of gray on the engine surface are more noticeable. There are literally thousands of rivets holding together this wing and its engine together.

The size of the wing dwarfs the clouds beyond while entire aircrafts I see from a distance mark but little spots in the vastness of the sky. The only tangible evidence of the reversal in one's perception of the wing as opposed to the clouds extending towards the horizon is punctuated through the occasional and gentle shaking of the wing upon encountering an air-pocket.

One thinks that the giant and merciful reach of nature taps the plane ever so gently, every now and then, reminding one of the imbalance of power between these actors. There is an indescribable logic that brings the harmonious and the antagonistic together making the sky and the airplane's wing dance in unison.

By travelling from Dhahran to New York, through Ankara, I am transitioning from a brief experience as a visitor of the Saudi culture to my emigre culture as a US citizen, by way of my native Turkish culture.

Once again, there is an indescribable logic that brings the harmonious and the antagonistic together making the inner, Turkish way of being, dance gracefully with my outer, US way of being, tested at every turn by the rhythmic sounds of the Saudi *takmir*-drum.

You can get the following titles by the same author from Amazon

Hermit Crab, 2017.

This is a tale of how prejudice can ruin lives and how with persistence and a little serendipity love can triumph in the end. Edward Amado is in a bind. He needs a new improved Ed and to achieve this as inconspicuously as possible. This makes for a family suspense case unbeknownst to his wife Kay and son Jay: "When I let go of what I am, I become what I might be."

https://www.amazon.com/Hermit-Crab-Illustrated-Sail-Anon/dp/097629415X/ref=sr_1_2?ie=UTF8&qid=151490893 8&sr=8-2&keywords=hermit+crab+sail+anon

Musings of a Male Menopausal Mutt, 2017.

This is a collection of poems recalling the Menopausal Mutt's musings about encounters with historical characters like Aristoteles, Cadmus, Julius Caesar:, Cicero, Dionysus, René Descartes, Alexandre Dumas, Elvis, Herodotus, William of Ockham, Plato, Socrates, Spinoza, and Zeus.

https://www.amazon.com/Musings-Male-Menopausal-Mutt-Collection/dp/0976294192/ref=sr_1_1?s=books&ie=UTF8&qi d=1514909041&sr=1-1&keywords=musings+of+a+male+ sail+anon